# Practical Guide to Ionic 2

## Practical Guide

A. De Quattro

# Practical Guide

**1. Introduction**

## Introduction to Ionic 2

### What is Ionic?

Ionic is an open-source framework for developing hybrid mobile applications. Its main feature is the ability to create applications that run across multiple platforms (iOS, Android, and the web) using a single codebase written in HTML, CSS, and JavaScript. This hybrid approach contrasts with native applications, which must be developed separately for each platform using specific programming languages such as Swift for iOS and Kotlin or Java for Android.

The core of Ionic is based on Angular, one of the most popular JavaScript frameworks for building web applications. Thanks to this integration, Ionic leverages Angular's capabilities to create rich and dynamic user interfaces. In addition to Angular, Ionic uses Apache Cordova, a platform that provides access to native device APIs (such as the camera, geolocation, and notification system) through JavaScript, thus enabling the development of features typically reserved for native apps.

Ionic 2 is the second major version of the framework, released in 2016, representing a significant advancement over the first version. This update was designed to take advantage of the improvements introduced by Angular 2, including enhanced performance, a new programming syntax, and support for TypeScript, a superset of JavaScript that introduces static typing, making the code more robust and maintainable.

### History and Evolution of Ionic

Ionic was originally created by Max Lynch, Ben Sperry, and Adam Bradley of Drifty Co., a small startup founded in 2012. Their goal was to make mobile app development more accessible to web developers by using familiar web technologies like HTML, CSS, and JavaScript. The first version of Ionic was released in 2013 and was based on AngularJS, the original version of Angular.

As web and mobile technologies evolved, Ionic continued to advance. In 2016, with the release of Angular 2, which introduced a completely new architecture compared to the previous version, the Ionic team decided to rewrite the framework from scratch, leading to the creation of Ionic 2. This new version not only integrated Angular 2's innovations but also brought numerous improvements in terms of performance, usability, and multi-platform support.

Ionic 2 introduced a new navigation system, based on a stack concept similar to that used in native applications, and a new rendering engine that significantly improved app performance, especially on older mobile devices. Additionally, support for TypeScript allowed developers to write more secure and maintainable code.

After Ionic 2, the framework continued to evolve, with subsequent versions further enhancing integration with Angular, access to native APIs, and support for other technologies like React and Vue.js. Today, Ionic is one of the most popular frameworks for hybrid mobile app development, used by millions of developers worldwide.

### System Requirements

To start developing applications with Ionic 2, you need to set up your development environment. Below are the minimum system requirements to install and use Ionic 2:

1. **Operating System**: You can develop with Ionic on Windows, macOS, and Linux. However, for iOS app development, you need a Mac with macOS, as the tools required to

build and test iOS apps (such as Xcode) are only available on this platform.

2. **Node.js and npm**: Ionic requires Node.js, a JavaScript runtime environment that allows you to run JavaScript code outside the browser. Along with Node.js, npm (Node Package Manager) is installed, which is necessary for managing dependencies and installing packages, including Ionic itself.

3. **Ionic CLI**: The Ionic Command Line Interface (CLI) is an essential tool for creating, developing, and deploying Ionic applications. The CLI is a Node.js application, so Node.js must be installed on the system.

4. **Code Editor**: While you can use any text editor to write Ionic code, it is recommended to use an advanced code editor like Visual Studio Code, which offers many useful features for development, such as TypeScript support, integrated debugging, and a wide range of extensions.

5. **Git**: Although not strictly necessary, it is highly recommended to install Git, a distributed version control system, to manage source code and collaborate with other developers.

### Installation and Configuration

#### Installing Node.js and npm

The first step to setting up your development environment for Ionic 2 is to install Node.js and npm. Node.js is available for all major platforms (Windows, macOS, and Linux) and can be downloaded from the official Node.js website (https://nodejs.org/). npm is installed automatically along with Node.js.

Here are the steps to install Node.js:

1. Visit the official Node.js website and download the installer appropriate for your

operating system.

2. Follow the installer instructions to complete the installation.

3. After installation, open a terminal (or Command Prompt on Windows) and type `node -v` to verify that Node.js has been installed correctly. This command should return the installed version of Node.js.

4. Also verify the installation of npm with the command `npm -v`, which will return the version of npm.

#### Installing Ionic CLI

Once Node.js and npm are installed, the next step is to install the Ionic CLI. The CLI is a command-line interface that facilitates the creation, development, and management of Ionic projects.

To install the Ionic CLI, run the following command in the terminal:

```bash
npm install -g @ionic/cli
```

The `-g` option indicates that the Ionic CLI will be installed globally, making it accessible from any directory on your system.

After installation, you can verify that the CLI has been installed correctly by running:

```bash
ionic --version
```

This command will return the version of the Ionic CLI installed.

#### Creating the First Ionic Project

Now that you have installed the Ionic CLI, you are ready to create your first Ionic project. The Ionic CLI includes a simple command to generate a new project with a basic structure and necessary dependencies.

To create a new project, run the following command:

```bash
ionic start myFirstApp tabs
```

In this command, `myFirstApp` is the project name, and `tabs` is the base template used to create the project. Ionic offers several predefined templates such as `blank`, `tabs`, `sidemenu`, etc., each with a different initial configuration. The `tabs` template, for example, creates an app with a preconfigured tab-based navigation.

During the execution of the command, the CLI will ask if you want to integrate the project with Capacitor, a tool that allows you to easily add native functionality to your app. If you are new to Ionic, you can select "No" and add Capacitor later if needed.

Once the project creation is complete, you can navigate to the project directory and run the app with the command:

```bash
cd myFirstApp
ionic serve
```

This command will start a local development server and open the app in the browser. Any changes to the source code will be automatically reflected in the browser, thanks to live-reloading support.

#### Ionic Project Structure

A newly created Ionic project has a predefined directory structure that may seem complex at first glance, but it is well-organized to facilitate the development and maintenance of the application. Here is an overview of the main directories and files you will find in an Ionic 2 project:

1. **`src/`**: This is the main source code directory for the app. It contains all the application files, including components, pages, services, and static resources.

   - **`app/`**: Contains the main application module (`app.module.ts`), the root component (`app.component.ts`), and the route configuration file (`app-routing.module.ts`).

   - **`assets/`**: Contains static resources for the app, such as images, audio files, fonts, etc. Files in this directory are included directly in the final app package.

- **`environments/`**: Contains configuration files specific to different environments (development, production, etc.). These files can be used to manage settings such as API endpoints, third-party keys, and other environment variables.

- **`pages/`**: This directory contains the components for the application's pages. Each page typically consists of three files: a TypeScript file (`.ts`) for the page's logic, an HTML file (`.html`) for the layout, and a CSS or SCSS file (`.scss`) for styling.

- **`theme/`**: Contains global style files for the application. The main file is `variables.scss`, where you can define SCSS variables for colors, fonts, and other style properties that can be reused throughout the project.

2. **`www/`**: This directory is automatically generated during the build process and contains the final packaged version of the app, ready for distribution. Typically, you should not modify files directly in this directory.

3. **`node_modules/`**: Contains all project dependencies installed via npm. This directory is created automatically during dependency installation and should not be modified manually.

4. **`package.json`**: This file contains project information and its dependencies, as well as scripts for common tasks such as starting the development server, running tests, and building the project.

5. **`ionic.config.json`**: This configuration file contains Ionic-specific settings for the project, such as the project name, output directory, and other configuration options.

6. **`tsconfig.json`**: TypeScript configuration file, defining compilation options for the language, such as type checking levels and supported JavaScript versions.

7. **`capacitor.config.json`**: If you have integrated Capacitor into your project, this file contains Capacitor-specific configuration, such as the bundle ID and output directories for native builds.

This structure is designed to be modular and scalable,

allowing for logical and maintainable organization of code as the application grows.

## 2.Architecture of Ionic 2

Ionic 2 is designed to make the creation of hybrid mobile applications a straightforward and efficient process. One of the key aspects that contribute to this simplicity is its architecture, which is based on the concepts of Components, Pages, and Modules. These concepts, along with the application lifecycle and dependency management, are fundamental for understanding how to develop and maintain an Ionic application. In this context, we will explore how to create user interfaces using HTML and CSS in Ionic, utilizing basic UI components and ensuring that the design is responsive and mobile-first.

### Understanding Components, Pages, and Modules

#### Components

In Ionic 2, a **Component** is one of the

fundamental units of the architecture. A component represents a portion of the user interface and contains the associated presentation logic. Components are reusable and can be combined to form the complete interface of the application. A component typically includes:

- **HTML Template**: Defines the structure and layout of the component.

- **CSS or SCSS**: Defines the style of the component.

- **TypeScript (TS)**: Contains the logic and behavior of the component.

An example of a simple component might be a custom button:

```typescript
import { Component } from '@angular/core';
```

```
@Component({
  selector: 'custom-button',
  template: `
    <button [style.background-color]="color"
(click)="onClick()">
      <ng-content></ng-content>
    </button>
  `,
  styles: [`
    button {
      padding: 10px 20px;
      font-size: 16px;
      border: none;
      border-radius: 5px;
      cursor: pointer;
    }
  `]
})
```

```
export class CustomButtonComponent {
  color: string = 'blue';

  onClick() {
    console.log('Button clicked!');
  }
}
```

In this example, `CustomButtonComponent` is a component that can be reused in different parts of the application. The component accepts dynamic content (via `ng-content`) and applies a default style to the button.

#### Pages

**Pages** in Ionic are special components that represent entire screens of the application. A page is a fully-fledged component but is managed through Ionic's navigation system, which allows transitioning from one page to another and managing the application's state.

An example of a page might be a login screen:

```typescript
import { Component } from '@angular/core';
import { NavController } from 'ionic-angular';

@Component({
  selector: 'page-login',
  templateUrl: 'login.html'
})
export class LoginPage {
  username: string;
  password: string;

  constructor(private navCtrl: NavController)
```

```
{}

  login() {
    if (this.username === 'admin' &&
this.password === 'password') {
      this.navCtrl.push('HomePage');
    } else {
      console.log('Invalid credentials');
    }
  }
}
```

Ionic's navigation system allows transitioning from `LoginPage` to `HomePage` using the `push` method, which adds `HomePage` to the navigation stack.

#### Modules

In Angular, a **Module** is a mechanism for logically grouping related components, directives, pipes, and services. Ionic 2 uses Angular modules to organize code in a scalable and maintainable manner. Every Ionic application has at least one module, the root module (`AppModule`), which defines the application’s startup.

Here is an example of a module in Ionic:

```typescript
import { NgModule } from '@angular/core';
import { IonicPageModule } from 'ionic-angular';
import { LoginPage } from './login';

@NgModule({
 declarations: [LoginPage],
 imports: [IonicPageModule.forChild(LoginPage)],
```

```
})

export class LoginPageModule {}
```

In this example, `LoginPageModule` is a module specific to the login page. By using `IonicPageModule.forChild(LoginPage)`, Ionic optimizes code management so that the page is loaded only when necessary (lazy loading), improving app performance.

### The Ionic Application Lifecycle

Every Ionic application follows a lifecycle closely tied to Angular's lifecycle. However, Ionic adds some specific hooks that help manage transitions between pages, component initialization, and other UI-related operations.

#### Lifecycle Hooks

The main lifecycle hooks in Ionic are:

1. **ionViewDidLoad**: Called once when the view has been loaded. It is useful for initializing data when the page is first displayed.

2. **ionViewWillEnter**: Called each time the page is about to become active. It is useful for updating data or preparing the UI.

3. **ionViewDidEnter**: Called when the page has become active and visible. It can be used to start animations or load dynamic data.

4. **ionViewWillLeave**: Called before the page leaves the active state. It can be used to stop animations or save states.

5. **ionViewDidLeave**: Called when the page has left the active state. Useful for cleaning up resources or canceling events.

6. **ionViewWillUnload**: Called when the view is about to be removed from navigation. It can be used to clean up resources or cancel timers.

An example of using lifecycle hooks in a page:

```typescript
import { Component } from '@angular/core';
import { NavController } from 'ionic-angular';

@Component({
  selector: 'page-home',
  templateUrl: 'home.html'
})
export class HomePage {
```

```
constructor(public navCtrl: NavController)
{}

ionViewWillEnter() {
  console.log('HomePage is about to become
active');
}

ionViewDidEnter() {
  console.log('HomePage has become
active');
}

ionViewWillLeave() {
  console.log('HomePage is about to leave
the active state');
}

ionViewDidLeave() {
```

console.log('HomePage has left the active state');

}

}

```

### Dependency Management

In an Angular application (and thus in Ionic), dependency management is a crucial aspect. Angular uses a **Dependency Injection (DI)** system that allows injecting dependencies (such as services) into components or other classes, making the code more modular and testable.

#### Providers and Services

**Services** in Angular/Ionic are classes that contain business logic and common operations that can be shared between different
```

components or pages. Services are registered as **Providers** in modules and can be injected into components or other services.

Here's an example of a service:

```typescript
import { Injectable } from '@angular/core';

@Injectable()
export class AuthService {
  private isAuthenticated: boolean = false;

  login(username: string, password: string): boolean {
    if (username === 'admin' && password === 'password') {
      this.isAuthenticated = true;
      return true;
```

```
    }
    return false;
  }

  logout() {
    this.isAuthenticated = false;
  }

  isLoggedIn(): boolean {
    return this.isAuthenticated;
  }
}
```

To use this service in a component:

```typescript
import { Component } from '@angular/core';
```

```
import { AuthService } from
'../services/auth.service';


@Component({
  selector: 'app-login',
  templateUrl: './login.component.html',
})
export class LoginComponent {


  constructor(private authService:
AuthService) {}


  login(username: string, password: string) {
    if (this.authService.login(username,
password)) {
      console.log('Login successful');
    } else {
      console.log('Login failed');
    }
```

```
  }
}
```

### Creating User Interfaces

#### Introduction to Using HTML and CSS in Ionic

Ionic 2 allows you to create user interfaces using standard web technologies like HTML and CSS, but with the addition of Angular directives and components for enhanced interactivity and advanced functionality.

#### Basic Structure of an HTML Template in Ionic

In an Ionic app, HTML templates define the structure of the user interface. For example, here is a simple template for a login page:

```html
<ion-header>
  <ion-navbar>
    <ion-title>Login</ion-title>
  </ion-navbar>
</ion-header>

<ion-content padding>
  <ion-list>
    <ion-item>
      <ion-label floating>Username</ion-label>
      <ion-input type="text"
[(ngModel)]="username"></ion-input>
    </ion-item>
    <ion-item>
      <ion-label floating>Password</ion-label>
      <ion-input type="password"
[(ngModel)]="password"></ion-input>
```

```
    </ion-item>
  </ion-list>
  <button ion-button block
(click)="login()">Login</button>
</ion-content>
```

This template uses Ionic components such as `ion-header`, `ion-navbar`, `ion-title`, `ion-content`, `ion-list`, `ion-item`, `ion-label`, and `ion-input` to build a simple login interface.

#### Introduction to SCSS

Ionic uses **SCSS** (Sass), an extension of CSS that allows the use of variables, nested rules, mixins, and other advanced features. This makes it easier to manage complex styles and maintain a consistent design.

An example of using SCSS in an Ionic app:

```scss
// theme/variables.scss
$primary-color: #3880ff;
$secondary-color: #0cd1e8;
$text-color: #222;

body {
  font-family: 'Roboto', sans-serif;
  color: $text-color;
}

button {
  background-color: $primary-color;
  color: #fff;
  &:hover {
    background-color: darken($primary-color, 10%);
```

```
  }
}
```

### Basic UI Components

Ionic 2 provides a wide range of ready-to-use UI components that simplify the creation of modern, responsive user interfaces. Some of the most common components include buttons, lists, inputs, and cards.

#### Buttons

Buttons are an essential element in any application. Ionic allows the creation

of styled buttons with the `ion-button` component.

```html
<button ion-button color="primary"
(click)="doSomething()">Primary
Button</button>

<button ion-button outline
color="secondary">Secondary
Button</button>
```

In this example, buttons can have predefined colors such as `primary` and `secondary`, and can be styled with borders (`outline`).

#### Lists

Lists are used to display lists of data. Ionic provides `ion-list` and `ion-item` for creating lists.

```html
<ion-list>
```

```
 <ion-item *ngFor="let item of items">
   {{ item.name }}
 </ion-item>
</ion-list>
```

This example uses `ngFor` to iterate over an array of items and display each in a list.

#### Input

Input fields are crucial for interactive applications. Ionic offers various types of inputs such as `text`, `password`, `email`, etc.

```html
<ion-item>
  <ion-label floating>Email</ion-label>
  <ion-input type="email"
```

```
[(ngModel)]="email"></ion-input>

</ion-item>

<ion-item>

  <ion-label floating>Password</ion-label>

  <ion-input type="password"
[(ngModel)]="password"></ion-input>

</ion-item>
```

This example shows a simple login form with `email` and `password` fields.

### Responsiveness and Mobile-First Design

One of Ionic's main features is support for responsiveness, meaning that applications are designed to automatically adapt to different screen sizes, ensuring an optimal user experience on mobile devices, tablets, and desktops.

#### Grid System

Ionic provides a flexible grid system based on CSS Grid, which allows the creation of complex and responsive layouts.

```html
<ion-grid>
  <ion-row>
    <ion-col size="6">Column 1</ion-col>
    <ion-col size="6">Column 2</ion-col>
  </ion-row>
  <ion-row>
    <ion-col size="12" size-sm="6">Column 3</ion-col>
    <ion-col size="12" size-sm="6">Column 4</ion-col>
  </ion-row>
```

```
</ion-grid>
```

In this example, columns adjust their size based on the screen size using size classes (`size`, `size-sm`).

#### Media Queries

In addition to the grid system, you can use media queries in SCSS to apply specific styles to different screen resolutions.

```scss
.container {
 padding: 20px;

 @media (min-width: 768px) {
  padding: 40px;
```

```
  }

  @media (min-width: 1024px) {
    padding: 60px;
  }
}
```

This example increases the padding of `.container` as the screen width increases, improving readability on larger devices.

### Using Icons and Typography

#### Icons

Ionic includes a set of predefined icons called **Ionicons**, which are easily integrated into HTML templates.

```html
<ion-icon name="home"></ion-icon>

<ion-icon name="star"
color="primary"></ion-icon>
```

Icons can be used as standalone elements or within buttons and lists.

#### Typography

Typography in Ionic is primarily managed through SCSS, allowing for the use of different font families, sizes, and weights.

```scss
body {

  font-family: 'Lato', sans-serif;
```

```
  line-height: 1.5;
}

h1, h2, h3, h4, h5, h6 {
  font-weight: 700;
}
```

This example uses a custom font (`Lato`) and applies a consistent style to headings (`h1, h2, h3, h4, h5, h6`).

The architecture of Ionic 2, based on Components, Pages, and Modules, along with dependency management and the application lifecycle, provides a solid foundation for developing powerful and flexible hybrid mobile applications. Creating user interfaces with Ionic is made simple by using ready-to-use UI components, supporting responsiveness, and adopting a mobile-first design. This combination of tools and concepts enables the development of modern, responsive, and scalable applications with a single codebase for multiple platforms.

## 3.Navigation and Routing in Ionic 2

Navigation and routing are fundamental elements for developing modern mobile applications. In Ionic 2, these concepts are managed through an integrated routing system based on Angular. This system allows for navigation between different pages of the application, passing data between them, and handling complex navigation scenarios. In this document, we will explore in detail the routing system of Ionic 2, how to implement navigation between pages, pass data between them, and manage advanced navigation.

### Introduction to Ionic 2 Routing System

The routing system in Ionic 2 is based on Angular’s router, which allows defining routes and managing navigation between pages. A route in this context is a mapping between a URL and a component of the application. When a user navigates to a specific URL, Angular's router loads the corresponding component and displays it in the user interface.

Defining Routes

In Ionic 2, routes are defined in the app-routing.module.ts file, located in the main folder of the application. Here is an example of how to define routes for an application:

typescript

Copia codice

```
import { NgModule } from '@angular/core';

import { PreloadAllModules, RouterModule, Routes } from '@angular/router';


const routes: Routes = [

  { path: '', redirectTo: 'home', pathMatch: 'full' },

  { path: 'home', loadChildren: () => import('./home/home.module').then(m => m.HomePageModule) },

  { path: 'about', loadChildren: () => import('./about/about.module').then(m => m.AboutPageModule) },
```

```
  { path: 'contact', loadChildren: () =>
import('./contact/contact.module').then(m =>
m.ContactPageModule) },

];


@NgModule({

  imports: [RouterModule.forRoot(routes,
{ preloadingStrategy: PreloadAllModules })],

  exports: [RouterModule]

})

export class AppRoutingModule { }
```

In this example, we have defined three main routes:

home: The route that loads the main page module (HomePageModule).

about: The route that loads the "About" page module (AboutPageModule).

contact: The route that loads the "Contact" page module (ContactPageModule).

The use of loadChildren is an example of lazy loading, which allows modules to be loaded only when needed, improving application performance.

Configuring the Router

Angular's router provides various options for configuring route behavior. For example, the preloadingStrategy option used above allows preloading modules, reducing load times when the user navigates to a new page.

typescript

Copia codice

```
@NgModule({
  imports: [RouterModule.forRoot(routes,
{ preloadingStrategy: PreloadAllModules })],
  exports: [RouterModule]
})
```

Additionally, route guards can be defined to control access to certain routes. Guards can be used to protect pages that require authentication or specific permissions.

## Implementing Navigation Between Pages

Once routes are defined, the next step is to implement navigation between different pages of the application. Ionic 2 offers several ways to navigate between pages using the NavController service or Angular router links.

### Navigation Using NavController

The NavController service is one of the primary classes used to manage navigation in Ionic applications. This service provides methods to transition from one page to another, return to the previous page, and manage the navigation stack.

Here's an example of how to navigate from one page to another using NavController:

typescript

Copia codice

```
import { Component } from '@angular/core';
import { NavController } from 'ionic-angular';

@Component({
  selector: 'page-home',
  templateUrl: 'home.html'
})
export class HomePage {

  constructor(public navCtrl: NavController)
{}

  goToAboutPage() {
    this.navCtrl.push('AboutPage');
  }
}
```

In this example, the push method is used to navigate to the "AboutPage". push adds the new page to the navigation stack, allowing the user to return to the previous page using the back button.

## Navigation Using RouterLink

Another way to handle navigation is by using Angular's RouterLink directly in the HTML template. This method is more familiar to those who have experience with traditional web development.

Here's an example of using RouterLink in a template:

html

Copia codice

```html
<ion-button [routerLink]="['/about']">
  Go to About Page
</ion-button>
```

In this case, the ion-button is linked to the /about route using the [routerLink] attribute.

When the user clicks the button, Angular's router handles the navigation to the corresponding page.

Programmatic Navigation with Router

An alternative to using NavController is to use Angular's router for programmatic navigation. This approach is useful in more complex applications where precise control over navigation is needed.

Here's an example of programmatic navigation using Router:

typescript

Copia codice

```
import { Component } from '@angular/core';
import { Router } from '@angular/router';

@Component({
```

```
  selector: 'page-home',
  templateUrl: 'home.html'
})
export class HomePage {

  constructor(private router: Router) {}

  goToAboutPage() {
    this.router.navigate(['/about']);
  }
}
```

In this example, router.navigate(['/about']) is used to navigate to the "About" page. This method allows navigation between pages without altering the Ionic navigation stack.

## Passing Data Between Pages

In many applications, it is necessary to pass data from one page to another during navigation. Ionic 2 offers several methods for achieving this, using either the NavController of Ionic or Angular's Router.

Passing Data with NavController

When using NavController, data can be passed between pages using an object as a second argument to the push method. This data can be retrieved on the destination page using NavParams.

Here's an example:

Source Page (HomePage):

typescript

Copia codice

```
import { Component } from '@angular/core';
import { NavController } from 'ionic-angular';
@Component({
 selector: 'page-home',
```

```
  templateUrl: 'home.html'
})
export class HomePage {

  constructor(public navCtrl: NavController)
{}

  goToDetailPage() {
    this.navCtrl.push('DetailPage', { id: 42,
name: 'John Doe' });
  }
}
```

Destination Page (DetailPage):

typescript

Copia codice

```
import { Component } from '@angular/core';
import { NavParams } from 'ionic-angular';
```

```
@Component({
  selector: 'page-detail',
  templateUrl: 'detail.html'
})
export class DetailPage {

  id: number;
  name: string;

  constructor(private navParams: NavParams)
{
    this.id = navParams.get('id');
    this.name = navParams.get('name');
  }
}
```

In this example, HomePage passes an object containing an id and a name to DetailPage. DetailPage retrieves these data using NavParams.

## Passing Data with Router

When using Angular's router, data can be passed via query parameters or route parameters.

Here's an example using query parameters:

Source Page (HomePage):

typescript

Copia codice

```
import { Component } from '@angular/core';
import { Router } from '@angular/router';

@Component({
  selector: 'page-home',
  templateUrl: 'home.html'
})
export class HomePage {
```

```
  constructor(private router: Router) {}


  goToDetailPage() {
    this.router.navigate(['/detail'],
{ queryParams: { id: 42, name: 'John
Doe' } });
  }
}
```

Destination Page (DetailPage):

typescript

Copia codice

```
import { Component, OnInit } from
'@angular/core';
import { ActivatedRoute } from
'@angular/router';


@Component({
```

```
  selector: 'page-detail',
  templateUrl: 'detail.html'
})
export class DetailPage implements OnInit {

  id: number;
  name: string;

  constructor(private route: ActivatedRoute)
{}

  ngOnInit() {
    this.route.queryParams.subscribe(params
=> {
      this.id = params['id'];
      this.name = params['name'];
    });
  }
}
```

In this example, HomePage passes id and name as query parameters to DetailPage. DetailPage retrieves these values using ActivatedRoute.

Passing Data with Route Parameters

Route parameters are another way to pass data between pages. These are part of the URL and are defined in the route configuration.

Here's an example:

Route Configuration:

typescript

Copia codice

```
const routes: Routes = [
  { path: 'detail/:id/:name', loadChildren: () => import('./detail/detail.module').then(m => m.DetailPageModule) }
```

];

Source Page (HomePage):

typescript

Copia codice

```
import { Component } from '@angular/core';
import { Router } from '@angular/router';

@Component({
  selector: 'page-home',
  templateUrl: 'home.html'
})
export class HomePage {

  constructor(private router: Router) {}

  goToDetailPage() {
    this.router.navigate(['/detail', 42, 'John
```

Doe']);

  }

}

Destination Page (DetailPage):

typescript

Copia codice

```
import { Component, OnInit } from
'@angular/core';

import { ActivatedRoute } from
'@angular/router';


@Component({

 selector: 'page-detail',

 templateUrl: 'detail.html'

})

export class DetailPage implements OnInit {


 id: number;
```

```
 name: string;


 constructor(private route: ActivatedRoute)
{}


 ngOnInit() {
   this.route.params.subscribe(params => {
     this.id = params['id'];
     this.name = params['name'];
   });
 }
}
```

In this example, the id and name are passed as part of the URL path. DetailPage retrieves these values using ActivatedRoute.

## Advanced Navigation Techniques

For more complex scenarios, Ionic 2 provides advanced navigation techniques. These include navigating to a specific page in the stack, removing pages from the stack, and more.

## Navigating to a Specific Page in the Stack

You can navigate to a specific page in the navigation stack using the setRoot method. This method replaces the current page with a new one and clears the navigation stack.

typescript

Copia codice

```
this.navCtrl.setRoot('HomePage');
```

## Removing Pages from the Stack

If you need to remove a specific page from the navigation stack, you can use the remove method provided by NavController.

typescript

Copia codice

```
let index =
```

```
this.navCtrl.indexOf('ContactPage');
if (index > -1) {
  this.navCtrl.remove(index);
}
```

Handling Deep Links

Deep linking allows users to navigate directly to a specific page within the application using a URL. This is particularly useful for web-based Ionic applications or when integrating with third-party services.

Here's how to set up a deep link in Ionic 2:

typescript

Copia codice

```
const routes: Routes = [
  { path: 'home', component: HomePage },
  { path: 'detail/:id', component: DetailPage },
];
```

When the user navigates to https://example.com/detail/42, the application loads DetailPage and passes 42 as the id parameter.

Understanding the navigation and routing system in Ionic 2 is essential for developing powerful and user-friendly mobile applications. Whether you are navigating between pages, passing data, or handling complex scenarios, Ionic 2's integration with Angular's router provides a robust and flexible solution.

# 4.Managing Application State in Ionic 2

State management is one of the crucial aspects of modern application development, especially for those based on frameworks like Angular, which Ionic 2 is built upon. Understanding how to maintain, update, and synchronize the application state is essential to ensure that information remains consistent and available throughout the application.

In this article, we will explore state management in Ionic 2 in detail, including the use of services for state management, integration with Angular Services, and the creation and use of custom providers. We will see how to use these tools to build robust and modular applications with efficient and scalable state management.

### Using Services for State Management

In Angular, and thus in Ionic 2, services are

one of the main solutions for managing the global state of the application. Services allow data and functionality to be shared between different components without having to manually pass information between child and parent components. Services can maintain the application state, such as user authentication, user preferences, or temporary data needed for the application's operation.

#### Creating a State Service

To start, let's see how to create a simple service in Ionic 2 to manage the application state. For example, let's assume we want to manage the state of an authenticated user.

1. **Creating the service:**

```typescript
import { Injectable } from '@angular/core';
```

```
@Injectable({
  providedIn: 'root'
})
export class AuthService {
  private isLoggedIn: boolean = false;
  private userData: any = null;

  constructor() {}

  login(userData: any): void {
    this.isLoggedIn = true;
    this.userData = userData;
  }

  logout(): void {
    this.isLoggedIn = false;
    this.userData = null;
  }
```

```
  getIsLoggedIn(): boolean {
    return this.isLoggedIn;
  }

  getUserData(): any {
    return this.userData;
  }
}
```

In this example, `AuthService` manages the user's authentication state. The service contains methods to perform login, logout, and get the current user state.

2. **Injecting the service into components:**

To use the service in a component, we need to

inject the service into the component's constructor. For example:

```typescript
import { Component } from '@angular/core';
import { AuthService } from
'../services/auth.service';

@Component({
  selector: 'app-login',
  templateUrl: './login.page.html',
  styleUrls: ['./login.page.scss'],
})
export class LoginPage {

  constructor(private authService:
AuthService) {}

  onLogin() {
```

```
    const userData = { name: 'John Doe', email: 'john.doe@example.com' };
    this.authService.login(userData);
  }
}
```

In this case, `LoginPage` uses `AuthService` to manage authentication. When the user logs in, their data is stored in the service.

3. **Sharing state between components:**

Now, let's assume we want to access the authenticated user's data in another component, such as the `ProfilePage` component:

```typescript
import { Component, OnInit } from
```

```
'@angular/core';
import { AuthService } from
'../services/auth.service';


@Component({
  selector: 'app-profile',
  templateUrl: './profile.page.html',
  styleUrls: ['./profile.page.scss'],
})
export class ProfilePage implements OnInit {

  userData: any;

  constructor(private authService:
AuthService) {}

  ngOnInit() {
    this.userData =
this.authService.getUserData();
```

```
  }
}
```

In `ProfilePage`, we retrieve the user's data via the `getUserData` method of `AuthService`. This approach ensures that the user's data is available throughout the entire lifecycle of the application.

### Integration with Angular Services

Ionic 2, being built on Angular, fully leverages Angular's powerful service system. Angular services are ideal for state management since they are singletons by default, meaning only one instance of the service is created for the entire application unless specified otherwise.

#### Creating Complex Services

Angular services can be more complex and may include managing data from external sources, such as REST APIs, or interacting with other Angular services like HttpClient.

For example, let's create a service that manages products in an e-commerce application, fetching data from an external API:

1. **Creating the `ProductService`:**

```typescript
import { Injectable } from '@angular/core';
import { HttpClient } from '@angular/common/http';
import { Observable } from 'rxjs';

@Injectable({
  providedIn: 'root'
```

```
})
export class ProductService {
  private apiUrl =
'https://api.example.com/products';

  constructor(private http: HttpClient) {}

  getProducts(): Observable<any[]> {
    return this.http.get<any[]>(this.apiUrl);
  }

  getProductById(productId: number):
Observable<any> {
    return this.http.get<any>(`${this.apiUrl}/$
{productId}`);
  }
}
```

In this service, we use `HttpClient` to make

HTTP requests to the external API. `getProducts` returns an Observable containing the list of products, while `getProductById` returns the details of a single product.

2. **Using `ProductService` in a component:**

```typescript
import { Component, OnInit } from '@angular/core';
import { ProductService } from '../services/product.service';

@Component({
  selector: 'app-product-list',
  templateUrl: './product-list.page.html',
  styleUrls: ['./product-list.page.scss'],
})
```

```
export class ProductListPage implements OnInit {

  products: any[] = [];

  constructor(private productService: ProductService) {}

  ngOnInit() {
    this.productService.getProducts().subscribe(data => {
      this.products = data;
    });
  }
}
```

In `ProductListPage`, we use `ProductService` to obtain the list of products and display it on the page. We handle the data asynchronously using the Observable returned by `getProducts`.

3. **Managing state in combination with other services:**

A service can also manage state by interacting with other services. For example, we can have a `CartService` that uses `ProductService` to manage the products in the user's cart:

```typescript
import { Injectable } from '@angular/core';
import { ProductService } from './product.service';

@Injectable({
  providedIn: 'root'
})
```

```
export class CartService {
  private cartItems: any[] = [];

  constructor(private productService:
ProductService) {}

  addToCart(productId: number) {

this.productService.getProductById(productId
).subscribe(product => {
      this.cartItems.push(product);
    });
  }

  getCartItems(): any[] {
    return this.cartItems;
  }

  clearCart() {
```

```
    this.cartItems = [];
  }
}
```

In `CartService`, we use `ProductService` to obtain the details of the product to add to the cart and maintain the cart state in an array `cartItems`.

### Creating and Using Custom Providers

In addition to Angular's built-in services, it is possible to create **custom providers** to manage the application state. Custom providers are services that can be configured with specific dependencies or behaviors, offering a higher level of flexibility than simple services.

#### Creating a Custom Provider

To better understand the use of custom providers, let's create an example where we configure a service to manage user preferences with a provider that allows injecting a custom configuration.

1. **Creating the configuration interface:**

```typescript
export interface UserPreferencesConfig {
  theme: string;
  notificationsEnabled: boolean;
}
```

This interface defines the type of configuration that our `UserPreferencesService` will accept.

2. **Creating the `UserPreferencesService`:**

```typescript
import { Injectable, InjectionToken, Inject } from '@angular/core';

export const USER_PREFERENCES_CONFIG = new InjectionToken<UserPreferencesConfig>('user.preferences.config');

@Injectable({
  providedIn: 'root'
})
export class UserPreferencesService {
  private theme: string;
  private notificationsEnabled: boolean;

  constructor(@Inject(USER_PREFERENCES
```

```
_CONFIG) private config:
UserPreferencesConfig) {
    this.theme = config.theme;
    this.notificationsEnabled =
config.notificationsEnabled;
  }

  setTheme(theme: string): void {
    this.theme = theme;
  }

  getTheme(): string {
    return this.theme;
  }

  setNotificationsEnabled(enabled: boolean):
void {
    this.notificationsEnabled = enabled;
  }
```

```
  getNotificationsEnabled(): boolean {
    return this.notificationsEnabled;
  }
}
```

The `UserPreferencesService` manages user preferences. It uses an `InjectionToken` to inject the configuration when the service is created.

3. **Configuring the provider in the main module:**

```typescript
import { NgModule } from '@angular/core';
import { BrowserModule } from '@angular/platform-browser';
import { IonicModule } from
```

```
'@ionic/angular';

import { AppComponent } from
'./app.component';

import { AppRoutingModule } from './app-
routing.module';

import { UserPreferencesService,
USER_PREFERENCES_CONFIG } from
'./services/user-preferences.service';


@NgModule({

 declarations: [AppComponent],

 imports: [BrowserModule,
IonicModule.forRoot(), AppRoutingModule],

 providers: [

  { provide:
USER_PREFERENCES_CONFIG, useValue:
{ theme: 'dark', notificationsEnabled: true } },

  UserPreferencesService

 ],

 bootstrap: [AppComponent]
```

})

export class AppModule {}

```

In `AppModule`, we configure the `USER_PREFERENCES_CONFIG` provider with a default value. This value will be used by `UserPreferencesService`.

4. **Using the service in a component:**

```typescript

import { Component } from '@angular/core';

import { UserPreferencesService } from '../services/user-preferences.service';

@Component({

  selector: 'app-settings',

  templateUrl: './settings.page.html',

```
  styleUrls: ['./settings.page

.scss'],
})
export class SettingsPage {

  constructor(private userPreferencesService:
UserPreferencesService) {}

  toggleTheme() {
    const newTheme =
this.userPreferencesService.getTheme() ===
'dark' ? 'light' : 'dark';

this.userPreferencesService.setTheme(newThe
me);
  }

  toggleNotifications() {
    const enabled =
```

```
this.userPreferencesService.getNotificationsE
nabled();

this.userPreferencesService.setNotificationsEn
abled(!enabled);
  }
}
```

In `SettingsPage`, we use `UserPreferencesService` to manage user preferences, such as the application's theme and notification status.

### Conclusion

Managing application state in Ionic 2 is a crucial aspect of developing robust and scalable applications. By utilizing Angular services, integrating with HttpClient to handle remote data, and custom providers for advanced configurations, you can build applications that manage state efficiently and consistently.

Services allow centralizing the application's logic and sharing state between different components, reducing complexity and improving code maintainability. Custom providers also offer an additional level of flexibility, allowing services to be dynamically configured based on the application's specific needs.

Understanding and correctly implementing state management in Ionic 2 is fundamental to ensuring a smooth and responsive user experience, regardless of the application's complexity. With a solid foundation in state management principles, developers can confidently tackle the challenges of modern mobile development.

## 5.Application State Management in Ionic 2

Application state management is one of the most critical aspects of modern application development, especially when working with frameworks like Angular and Ionic 2. Effective state management is crucial for maintaining data consistency and ensuring that the user interface always reflects the current state of the application. In this section, we will explore the role of services in state management, integration with Angular Services, and the creation and use of custom providers.

#### Using Services for State Management

In Angular, and thus in Ionic 2, services are fundamental for managing the global state of the application. These services are used to maintain, update, and share state between different components of the application without needing to explicitly pass data through various component layers.

##### Creating a State Service

Suppose we want to create a task management application (todo app) where we need to maintain the state of a task list. We can create a service called `TodoService` to manage this state.

```typescript
import { Injectable } from '@angular/core';

@Injectable({
  providedIn: 'root'
})
export class TodoService {
  private todos: Array<{ id: number, title: string, completed: boolean }> = [];

  constructor() {}
```

```
 getTodos(): Array<{ id: number, title: string,
completed: boolean }> {

   return this.todos;

 }


 addTodo(title: string): void {

   const newTodo = {

     id: this.todos.length + 1,

     title,

     completed: false

   };

   this.todos.push(newTodo);

 }


 toggleTodoCompletion(id: number): void {

   const todo = this.todos.find(t => t.id ===
id);

   if (todo) {
```

```
      todo.completed = !todo.completed;
    }
  }

  removeTodo(id: number): void {
    this.todos = this.todos.filter(t => t.id !== id);
  }
}
```

In this example, `TodoService` maintains an array of objects representing tasks. It includes methods for adding new tasks, toggling completion status, and removing tasks.

##### Injecting the Service into Components

To use `TodoService` in a component, we need to inject the service into the component's constructor.

```typescript
import { Component } from '@angular/core';
import { TodoService } from
'../services/todo.service';

@Component({
  selector: 'app-todo-list',
  templateUrl: './todo-list.page.html',
  styleUrls: ['./todo-list.page.scss'],
})
export class TodoListPage {
  todos = [];

  constructor(private todoService:
TodoService) {}

  ngOnInit() {
```

```
    this.todos = this.todoService.getTodos();
  }

  addTodo(title: string) {
    this.todoService.addTodo(title);
    this.todos = this.todoService.getTodos();
  }

  toggleTodoCompletion(id: number) {
this.todoService.toggleTodoCompletion(id);
  }

  removeTodo(id: number) {
    this.todoService.removeTodo(id);
    this.todos = this.todoService.getTodos();
  }
}
```

```

`TodoListPage` is a component that uses `TodoService` to get the task list, add new tasks, and handle task completion and removal.

#### Integration with Angular Services

Integration with Angular Services is essential for extending application functionality and managing complex dependencies, such as backend interactions. Angular services are created as singletons and shared among all components that use them, making it easy to manage global state.

##### Using HttpClient for API Management

Suppose we want to fetch the task list from a remote server. We can extend `TodoService` to integrate `HttpClient`, an Angular service
```

used for making HTTP requests.

```typescript
import { Injectable } from '@angular/core';
import { HttpClient } from '@angular/common/http';
import { Observable } from 'rxjs';

@Injectable({
  providedIn: 'root'
})
export class TodoService {
  private todos: Array<{ id: number, title: string, completed: boolean }> = [];
  private apiUrl = 'https://api.example.com/todos';

  constructor(private http: HttpClient) {}
```

```
 fetchTodos(): Observable<any> {
  return this.http.get(this.apiUrl);
 }

 getTodos(): Array<{ id: number, title: string,
completed: boolean }> {
  return this.todos;
 }

 addTodo(title: string): void {
  const newTodo = {
   id: this.todos.length + 1,
   title,
   completed: false
  };
  this.todos.push(newTodo);
 }
```

```
  // ... Other methods
}
```

In this example, `TodoService` uses `HttpClient` to make a GET request to the API and fetch the task list. `fetchTodos` returns an Observable, which can be used in components to retrieve the data.

###### Using the Extended Service in Components

Now we can use `fetchTodos` in a component to load tasks when the component initializes.

```typescript
import { Component, OnInit } from '@angular/core';
import { TodoService } from '../services/todo.service';
```

```
@Component({
  selector: 'app-todo-list',
  templateUrl: './todo-list.page.html',
  styleUrls: ['./todo-list.page.scss'],
})
export class TodoListPage implements OnInit
{
  todos = [];


  constructor(private todoService:
TodoService) {}


  ngOnInit() {

this.todoService.fetchTodos().subscribe(data
=> {
      this.todos = data;
    });
```

```
  }

  // Other methods for managing tasks
}
```

In `ngOnInit`, the `TodoListPage` component uses `fetchTodos` to retrieve the task list from the server and update the user interface.

#### Creating and Using Custom Providers

Custom providers in Angular allow you to configure and create services based on specific needs, such as injecting custom configurations or creating service instances with specific dependencies.

##### Creating a Custom Provider

Suppose we want to configure a service to manage application settings, such as the user's preferred theme and language. We can create a custom provider to manage this configuration.

1. **Define the Configuration Interface:**

```typescript
export interface AppConfig {
  theme: string;
  language: string;
}
```

2. **Create the Configurable Service:**

```typescript
import { Injectable, InjectionToken, Inject }
from '@angular/core';
```

```
export const APP_CONFIG = new
InjectionToken<AppConfig>('app.config');

@Injectable({
  providedIn: 'root'
})
export class AppConfigService {
  private theme: string;
  private language: string;

  constructor(@Inject(APP_CONFIG) private
config: AppConfig) {
    this.theme = config.theme;
    this.language = config.language;
  }

  setTheme(theme: string): void {
    this.theme = theme;
```

```
}

getTheme(): string {
  return this.theme;
}

setLanguage(language: string): void {
  this.language = language;
}

getLanguage(): string {
  return this.language;
}
}
```

In this example, `AppConfigService` uses `InjectionToken` to inject a custom configuration object when the service is created.

3. **Configure the Provider in the Main Module:**

```typescript
import { NgModule } from '@angular/core';

import { BrowserModule } from '@angular/platform-browser';

import { IonicModule } from '@ionic/angular';

import { AppComponent } from './app.component';

import { AppRoutingModule } from './app-routing.module';

import { AppConfigService, APP_CONFIG } from './services/app-config.service';


@NgModule({

 declarations: [AppComponent],
```

```
  imports: [BrowserModule,
IonicModule.forRoot(), AppRoutingModule],

  providers: [

    { provide: APP_CONFIG, useValue:
{ theme: 'dark', language: 'en' } },

    AppConfigService

  ],

  bootstrap: [AppComponent]

})

export class AppModule {}
```

In `AppModule`, we configure `APP_CONFIG` with default values for theme and language. This provider will be used by `AppConfigService`.

4. **Using the Service in Components:**

```typescript
```

```
import { Component } from '@angular/core';
import { AppConfigService } from
'../services/app-config.service';


@Component({
  selector: 'app-settings',
  templateUrl: './settings.page.html',
  styleUrls: ['./settings.page.scss'],
})
export class SettingsPage {
  constructor(private appConfigService:
AppConfigService) {}


  changeTheme(newTheme: string) {

this.appConfigService.setTheme(newTheme);
  }


  changeLanguage(newLanguage: string) {
```

```
this.appConfigService.setLanguage(newLanguage);
  }
}
```

`SettingsPage` uses `AppConfigService` to change application settings like theme and language.

### Interaction with APIs and Data

Modern applications often require interaction with external APIs to fetch and send data. In Ionic 2, this interaction mainly occurs through `HttpClient`, which allows making HTTP requests and handling responses easily and effectively.

#### Introduction to API Calls

APIs (Application Programming Interfaces) allow applications to communicate with each other. RESTful APIs, based on the HTTP protocol, are among the most common in the context of web and mobile applications. Using `HttpClient`, we can perform various HTTP operations like GET, POST, PUT, and DELETE to interact with a server.

#### Using HttpClient in Ionic 2

`HttpClient` is a service provided by Angular that allows making HTTP requests. To use it in an Ionic 2 application, we first need to import and configure it in the main application module.

```typescript
import { HttpClientModule } from '@angular/common/http';

@NgModule({
```

```
 imports: [
   BrowserModule,
   IonicModule.forRoot(),
   AppRoutingModule,
   HttpClientModule // Importing HttpClientModule
 ],
 declarations: [AppComponent],
 bootstrap: [AppComponent]
})
export class AppModule {}
```

Now, we can inject `HttpClient` into a service or component and use it to make API calls

.

#### Fetching Data from an API

Let's modify our `TodoService` to fetch a list of todos from an API.

```typescript
import { Injectable } from '@angular/core';
import { HttpClient } from
'@angular/common/http';
import { Observable } from 'rxjs';

@Injectable({
 providedIn: 'root'
})
export class TodoService {
 private apiUrl =
'https://jsonplaceholder.typicode.com/todos';

 constructor(private http: HttpClient) {}
```

```typescript
 fetchTodos(): Observable<any> {
   return this.http.get(this.apiUrl);
 }
}
```

Here, `fetchTodos` makes a GET request to the API endpoint, returning an Observable that we can subscribe to in a component.

#### Displaying Fetched Data in the Component

```typescript
import { Component, OnInit } from '@angular/core';
import { TodoService } from '../services/todo.service';

@Component({
```

```
  selector: 'app-todo-list',
  templateUrl: './todo-list.page.html',
  styleUrls: ['./todo-list.page.scss'],
})
export class TodoListPage implements OnInit
{
  todos = [];


  constructor(private todoService:
TodoService) {}


  ngOnInit() {

this.todoService.fetchTodos().subscribe(data
=> {
      this.todos = data;
    });
  }
}
```

When `TodoListPage` initializes, it subscribes to the `fetchTodos` Observable, retrieves the data from the API, and displays it in the UI.

#### Handling Errors in API Calls

Error handling is crucial when interacting with APIs, as many things can go wrong (e.g., network issues, server errors).

To handle errors in `HttpClient` requests, we can use the `catchError` operator from RxJS.

```typescript
import { catchError } from 'rxjs/operators';

import { throwError } from 'rxjs';

fetchTodos(): Observable<any> {
```

```
  return this.http.get(this.apiUrl).pipe(
    catchError(error => {
      console.error('Error fetching todos', error);
      return throwError(error);
    })
  );
}
```

If an error occurs during the API call, it will be caught, logged, and rethrown for the component to handle.

### Summary

In this section, we explored the core concepts of application state management in Ionic 2 using Angular services. We discussed how to create and use services to manage application state, integrate Angular services like

`HttpClient` for API management, and create custom providers for configuration. Finally, we looked at how to handle interaction with APIs, fetch data, and manage errors effectively. These concepts are foundational for building robust, maintainable applications with Ionic 2.

**6.Storage and Local Data, Testing, and Debugging in Ionic 2**

Managing local data is a crucial aspect of mobile application development. In Ionic 2, there are various technologies and techniques for handling and storing data on the user's device, each with its characteristics and use cases. In this section, we will explore three main storage methods: SQLite, Local Storage, and IndexedDB.

#### Using SQLite with Ionic 2

SQLite is a lightweight and powerful SQL database engine that is very useful for mobile applications requiring complex data management. In Ionic 2, you can use SQLite via the `cordova-sqlite-storage` plugin.

##### Installation and Configuration

1. **Add the SQLite Plugin:**

First, you need to add the SQLite plugin to your Ionic 2 project. You can do this using the Cordova command:

```bash
ionic cordova plugin add cordova-sqlite-storage
npm install @ionic-native/sqlite
```

2. **Configure the SQLite Module:**

Import and configure the SQLite module in your main `app.module.ts` file.

```typescript
import { NgModule } from '@angular/core';
```

```
import { BrowserModule } from
'@angular/platform-browser';

import { IonicModule } from
'@ionic/angular';

import { AppComponent } from
'./app.component';

import { AppRoutingModule } from './app-
routing.module';

import { SQLite } from '@ionic-
native/sqlite/ngx';


@NgModule({

  declarations: [AppComponent],

  imports: [BrowserModule,
IonicModule.forRoot(), AppRoutingModule],

  providers: [

    SQLite

  ],

  bootstrap: [AppComponent]

})
```

```
export class AppModule {}
```

###### Creating and Managing the Database

1. **Service to Manage SQLite:**

Let's create a service to manage SQLite operations.

```typescript
import { Injectable } from '@angular/core';
import { SQLite, SQLiteObject } from '@ionic-native/sqlite/ngx';

@Injectable({
  providedIn: 'root'
})
export class DatabaseService {
```

```
private db: SQLiteObject;

constructor(private sqlite: SQLite) {}

public async initDB() {
  try {
    this.db = await this.sqlite.create({
      name: 'data.db',
      location: 'default'
    });
    await this.createTables();
  } catch (e) {
    console.error('Error initializing
database:', e);
  }
}

private async createTables() {
```

```
    try {
      await this.db.executeSql(`CREATE TABLE IF NOT EXISTS todos (
        id INTEGER PRIMARY KEY AUTOINCREMENT,
        title TEXT,
        completed INTEGER
      )`, []);
    } catch (e) {
      console.error('Error creating tables:', e);
    }
  }

  public async addTodo(title: string) {
    try {
      await this.db.executeSql('INSERT INTO todos (title, completed) VALUES (?, ?)', [title, 0]);
    } catch (e) {
```

```
      console.error('Error adding todo:', e);
    }
  }

  public async getTodos() {
    try {
      const res = await
this.db.executeSql('SELECT * FROM todos',
[]);
      let todos = [];
      for (let i = 0; i < res.rows.length; i++) {
        todos.push(res.rows.item(i));
      }
      return todos;
    } catch (e) {
      console.error('Error getting todos:', e);
    }
  }
}
```

```

2. **Using the Service in the Component:**

Now, you can use the service to interact with the SQLite database in a component.

```typescript
import { Component, OnInit } from '@angular/core';
import { DatabaseService } from '../services/database.service';

@Component({
  selector: 'app-todo-list',
  templateUrl: './todo-list.page.html',
  styleUrls: ['./todo-list.page.scss'],
})
export class TodoListPage implements
```
```

```
OnInit {
  todos = [];

  constructor(private dbService:
DatabaseService) {}

  async ngOnInit() {
    await this.dbService.initDB();
    this.todos = await
this.dbService.getTodos();
  }

  async addTodo() {
    await this.dbService.addTodo('New
Todo');
    this.todos = await
this.dbService.getTodos();
  }
}
```

```

#### Managing Local Storage

Local Storage is a simple web API for storing persistent key-value pairs on the client side. It is useful for storing small amounts of data, such as user preferences or temporary data.

##### Using Local Storage

Local Storage is accessible via `window.localStorage` and can be used directly in your components or services.

1. **Saving Data:**

```typescript
localStorage.setItem('userToken', 'abc123');
```
```

2. **Retrieving Data:**

```typescript
const userToken =
localStorage.getItem('userToken');
```

3. **Removing Data:**

```typescript
localStorage.removeItem('userToken');
```

4. **Clearing All Data:**

```typescript
localStorage.clear();
```

```

##### Example Usage in a Service

```typescript
import { Injectable } from '@angular/core';

@Injectable({
  providedIn: 'root'
})
export class AuthService {

  saveToken(token: string) {
    localStorage.setItem('authToken', token);
  }

  getToken(): string | null {
    return localStorage.getItem('authToken');

```
  }

  clearToken() {
    localStorage.removeItem('authToken');
  }
}
```

#### Introduction to IndexedDB

IndexedDB is a more advanced technology for storing structured data on the client side. It is more powerful than Local Storage and can handle large amounts of data and complex queries.

##### Using IndexedDB

1. **Creating and Opening a Database:**

```typescript
const request = indexedDB.open('myDatabase', 1);

request.onupgradeneeded = (event: any) => {
  const db = event.target.result;
  const objectStore = db.createObjectStore('todos', { keyPath: 'id', autoIncrement: true });
  objectStore.createIndex('title', 'title', { unique: false });
};

request.onsuccess = (event: any) => {
  const db = event.target.result;
  console.log('Database opened successfully:', db);
};
```

```
  request.onerror = (event: any) => {
    console.error('Database error:', event.target.errorCode);
  };
```

2. **Adding and Retrieving Data:**

```typescript
  function addTodo() {
    const request = indexedDB.open('myDatabase', 1);

    request.onsuccess = (event: any) => {
      const db = event.target.result;
      const transaction = db.transaction(['todos'], 'readwrite');
      const objectStore =
```

```
transaction.objectStore('todos');
    const requestAdd =
objectStore.add({ title: 'New Todo' });

    requestAdd.onsuccess = () => {
      console.log('Todo added successfully');
    };

    requestAdd.onerror = (event: any) => {
      console.error('Error adding todo:',
event.target.errorCode);
    };
  };
}

function getTodos() {
  const request =
indexedDB.open('myDatabase', 1);
```

```
    request.onsuccess = (event: any) => {
      const db = event.target.result;
      const transaction =
db.transaction(['todos'], 'readonly');
      const objectStore =
transaction.objectStore('todos');
      const requestGet = objectStore.getAll();

      requestGet.onsuccess = () => {
        console.log('Todos retrieved
successfully:', requestGet.result);
      };

      requestGet.onerror = (event: any) => {
        console.error('Error retrieving todos:',
event.target.errorCode);
      };
    };
  }
```

### Buttons and Menus in Ionic 2

Ionic 2 provides a range of ready-to-use UI components, such as buttons and menus, that help you build consistent and responsive user interfaces.

#### Components and Data Binding

##### Buttons

Buttons are essential elements in any application. In Ionic 2, buttons can be customized using style classes and directives.

```html
<ion-button color="primary">Click Me</ion-button>
```

```

You can also use the `(click)` directive to handle click events.

```html
<ion-button (click)="doSomething()">Click Me</ion-button>
```

In the TypeScript component:

```typescript
import { Component } from '@angular/core';

@Component({
 selector: 'app-home',
 templateUrl: 'home.page.html',
 styleUrls: ['home.page.scss'],

```
})
export class HomePage {
  doSomething() {
    console.log('Button clicked!');
  }
}
```

##### Menu

The menu in Ionic is created using the `ion-menu` component. Here is an example of a side menu:

```html
<ion-menu contentId="main-content">
  <ion-header>
    <ion-toolbar>
      <ion-title>Menu</ion-title>
```

```
    </ion-toolbar>
  </ion-header>
  <ion-content>
    <ion-list>
      <ion-item routerLink="/home">Home</ion-item>
      <ion-item routerLink="/settings">Settings</ion-item>
    </ion-list>
  </ion-content>
</ion-menu>

<ion-content id="main-content">
  <!-- Your main content goes here -->
</ion-content>
```

### Navigation in Ionic 2 Apps

Navigation between pages is a crucial part of any mobile application. Ionic 2 uses Angular Router to manage navigation and routing.

#### The Push Method and Its Parameters

The `push` method of the Ionic navigator is used to navigate to a new page.

```typescript
import { NavController } from
'@ionic/angular';

@Component

({
  selector: 'app-home',
  templateUrl: 'home.page.html',
  styleUrls: ['home.page.scss'],
```

```
})

export class HomePage {

  constructor(private navCtrl: NavController)
{}



  goToDetails() {

    this.navCtrl.navigateForward('/details');

  }

}
```

#### Passing Parameters

To pass parameters to a new page, you can use the `queryParams` property.

```typescript
import { NavController } from
'@ionic/angular';
```

```
@Component({
  selector: 'app-home',
  templateUrl: 'home.page.html',
  styleUrls: ['home.page.scss'],
})
export class HomePage {
  constructor(private navCtrl: NavController)
{}

  goToDetails() {
    this.navCtrl.navigateForward(['/details'], {
      queryParams: {
        data: 'test data'
      }
    });
  }
}
```

```

In the target page, you can retrieve the parameters using `ActivatedRoute`.

```typescript
import { Component, OnInit } from '@angular/core';
import { ActivatedRoute } from '@angular/router';

@Component({
  selector: 'app-details',
  templateUrl: './details.page.html',
  styleUrls: ['./details.page.scss'],
})
export class DetailsPage implements OnInit {
  data: string;

```
  constructor(private route: ActivatedRoute) {}

  ngOnInit() {
    this.route.queryParams.subscribe(params => {
      this.data = params['data'];
    });
  }
}
```

By leveraging these techniques and components, you can build robust, data-driven mobile applications with Ionic 2 that provide a smooth and responsive user experience.

# 7.Application Distribution in Ionic 2

Distributing a mobile application requires a series of specific steps to ensure the app is ready for publication on stores like Google Play and the App Store. In this guide, we will explore how to prepare your Ionic 2 application for distribution, create builds for Android and iOS, publish the app on stores, and finally, we will create a step-by-step example app to demonstrate the process.

### Preparation for Distribution

Before starting to distribute your application, it is essential to prepare it properly. This includes setting up the development environment, managing resources, configuring build settings, and verifying the app's quality.

#### 1. Setting Up the Development Environment

Make sure you have all the necessary tools installed and configured. These tools include:

- **Node.js and npm:** To manage project dependencies and necessary packages.
- **Ionic CLI and Cordova:** To manage the application's lifecycle and build creation.
- **Android Studio and Xcode:** For creating and managing builds for Android and iOS, respectively.

##### Installing Node.js and npm

Download and install Node.js from the official [Node.js](https://nodejs.org/) website. The installation of Node.js also includes npm (Node Package Manager), which will allow you to manage your project's dependencies.

##### Installing Ionic CLI and Cordova

Install Ionic CLI and Cordova globally using npm:

```bash
npm install -g @ionic/cli cordova
```

##### Installing Android Studio and Xcode

- **Android Studio:** Download and install [Android Studio](https://developer.android.com/studio) to develop and test Android applications. Configure the necessary SDK and build tools.
- **Xcode:** Download and install [Xcode](https://developer.apple.com/xcode/) from the Mac App Store to develop and test iOS applications.

#### 2. Configuring App Resources

The application's resources include icons and splash screens that must be configured to ensure a good user experience on various devices.

##### Managing Icons and Splash Screens

You can manage icons and splash screens through the following configuration files in the Ionic project:

- **`config.xml`:** This Cordova configuration file contains settings for icons and splash screens.

  Example of splash screen configuration:

```xml
<platform name="android">
  <splash src="res/screen/android/splash.png" density="port-hdpi"/>
```

```xml
    <!-- Other configurations -->
  </platform>

  <platform name="ios">
    <splash src="res/screen/ios/splash.png" width="320" height="480"/>
    <!-- Other configurations -->
  </platform>
```

- **Using the Cordova plugin to automatically generate resources:**

```bash
ionic cordova resources
```

#### 3. Configuring Build Settings

Before creating a final build, make sure to configure the build settings in the `config.xml` file and in `package.json`.

##### Example of `config.xml` Configuration

```xml
<widget id="com.example.app"
version="1.0.0"
xmlns="http://www.w3.org/ns/widgets">
  <name>MyApp</name>
  <description>An example app</description>
  <author email="support@example.com"
href="http://example.com">Example</author
>
  <preference name="android-
targetSdkVersion" value="29" />
  <preference name="ios-targetSdkVersion"
value="13.0" />
  <!-- Other configurations -->
</widget>
```

```

##### Configuring the `package.json` File

Ensure that dependency versions are updated and compatible.

### Creating Builds for Android and iOS

Once your application is prepared, you can start creating builds for the Android and iOS platforms. This process includes generating APKs (for Android) and IPAs (for iOS), which can be distributed and published on stores.

#### 1. Creating a Build for Android

1. **Configure Android Settings:**
```

Ensure that your Android environment is properly configured. This includes having a JDK installed and configured and Android Studio properly set up.

2. **Create a Debug Build:**

```bash
ionic cordova build android --debug
```

This command creates a debug build, useful for testing the app on an emulator or physical devicc.

3. **Create a Release Build:**

To prepare a release build, you first need to generate a signing key:

```bash
keytool -genkey -v -keystore my-release-key.keystore -alias alias_name -keyalg RSA -keysize 2048 -validity 10000
```

Then, create the release build:

```bash
ionic cordova build android --release
```

Sign the release APK:

```bash
jarsigner -verbose -sigalg SHA256withRSA -digestalg SHA-256 -keystore my-release-key.keystore platforms/android/app/build/outputs/apk/release/app-release-unsigned.apk alias_name
```

```

Align the APK:

```bash

zipalign -v 4 platforms/android/app/build/outputs/apk/release/app-release-unsigned.apk app-release.apk

```

#### 2. Creating a Build for iOS

1. **Configure iOS Settings:**

Open the iOS project in Xcode:

```bash

ionic cordova build ios

```
```

Then, open `platforms/ios/MyApp.xcworkspace` in Xcode.

2. **Create a Debug and Release Build:**

In Xcode, select the project target and configure the build type (Debug or Release). You can then create an app archive using the `Product > Archive` command.

3. **Signing and Distributing the IPA:**

After creating the archive, you can upload the IPA to App Store Connect for distribution.

### Publishing on the App Store and Google Play

Publishing the app on stores requires creating developer accounts and uploading the final builds.

#### 1. Publishing on Google Play

1. **Create a Google Play Developer Account:**

Register as a developer on [Google Play Console](https://play.google.com/console).

2. **Upload the APK to Google Play Console:**

Log in to Google Play Console and create a new application. Upload the signed APK file in the "Release Management" section.

3. **Complete App Information:**

Fill in the necessary information, such as description, screenshots, and app classification.

4. **Submit for Review:**

After completing all necessary information, submit the app for review. Google will perform a quality check before approving the app for publication.

#### 2. Publishing on the App Store

1. **Create an Apple Developer Account:**

Register as a developer on the [Apple Developer Program](https://developer.apple.com/programs/).

2. **Upload the IPA to App Store Connect:**

Use Xcode to upload the IPA to [App Store Connect](https://appstoreconnect.apple.com/).

3. **Complete App Information:**

Provide details such as description, screenshots, and app classification.

4. **Submit for Review:**

After completing all necessary information, submit the app for review. Apple will perform a quality check before approving the app for publication.

### Creating a Step-by-Step Example App

Let's create a simple example app to illustrate

the process of creation, building, and distribution.

#### 1. Project Creation

1. **Create a New Ionic Project:**

```bash
ionic start myApp blank
cd myApp
```

2. **Add Platforms:**

```bash
ionic cordova platform add android
ionic cordova platform add ios
```

#### 2. Adding Features

1. **Modify the Main Component:**

Update `src/app/home/home.page.html` to include a simple button.

```html
<ion-header>
  <ion-toolbar>
    <ion-title>
      My App
    </ion-title>
  </ion-toolbar>
</ion-header>

<ion-content>
```

```
    <ion-button (click)="showAlert()">Click Me!</ion-button>
  </ion-content>
```

Update `src/app/home/home.page.ts` to handle the button action.

```typescript
import { Component } from '@angular/core';
import { AlertController } from '@ionic/angular';

@Component({
  selector: 'app-home',
  templateUrl: './home.page.html',
  styleUrls: ['./home.page.scss'],
})
```

```
export class HomePage {

  constructor(public alertController: AlertController) {}

  async showAlert() {
    const alert = await this.alertController.create({
      header: 'Hello',
      subHeader: 'Ionic 2 App',
      message: 'You clicked the button!',
      buttons: ['OK']
    });

    await alert.present();
  }
}
```

#### 3. Testing the App

1. **Test Locally:**

```bash
ionic serve
```

2. **Test on Real Devices or Emulator:**

```bash
ionic cordova run android
ionic cordova run ios
```

#### 4. Creating the Build and Publishing

1. **Create the Release Build for Android:**

```bash
ionic cordova build android --release
```

2. **Create the Release Build for iOS:**

```bash
ionic cordova build ios --release
```

3. **Upload to the respective stores following the previous guidelines.**

### Conclusion

Distributing an application built with Ionic 2 requires careful preparation and build configuration to ensure a smooth distribution process. Preparing resources, configuring build settings, and following the publishing procedures on Google Play and the App Store are all crucial steps to ensure the success of your app.

With the creation of an example app, we have illustrated the process

from conception to distribution, providing a complete overview of how to develop, build, and publish Ionic 2 applications. By following these steps, you can ensure that your app is ready to be distributed and reach users on all major mobile platforms.

**Index**

www.ingramcontent.com/pod-product-compliance
Lightning Source LLC
Chambersburg PA
CBHW052203220526
45471CB00004B/1795

* 9 7 9 8 3 3 7 6 8 2 1 7 4 *